GOODBYE, CORN
Harvesting from Beginning to End

by

Tasha Ragel-Dial

the Peppertree Press

Sarasota, Florida

I dedicate this book to my Dad, Alan Ragel, who in my eyes,
will always be the best farmer in the world!

Love Forever & Ever,

Molly

PLEASE READ FIRST:

I made a promise to my Dad that I would one day write a short story based upon his farewell greeting, **Goodbye, Corn**. This was something he would say at the end of every harvest season from the time he was a young boy riding in the combine with his Dad, until his final harvest season with us. As the combine tore through its last field, cutting down the final rows, Dad would always say, **Goodbye, Corn** in a jovial, yet sincere tone.

I believe my Dad was grateful that harvest season was finally coming to a close, yet he understood until planting season next spring, the fields would remain bare. My Dad truly loved his profession and always honored its process. Farming was not just a job, but it was his way of life.

May the road rise up to meet you.

May the wind be always at your back.

May the sun shine warm upon your face;

the rains fall soft upon your fields and until we meet again,

may God hold you in the palm of His hand.

—Traditonal Gaelic Blessing

My Daddy is a farmer, he works hard everyday.
I'm a farmer's daughter, which I'm very proud to say!

Before you read this book, I think you need know,
it takes a lot of work to make a corn field grow.

First, certain chemicals go into the dirt.
Daddy's trained to use them, so he won't get hurt.

Next, what he does, to prepare for the seeds,
is break up the ground and tear out the weeds.

When it's time to plant the corn, the soil must be right.
This is why my Daddy works late into the night!

If the soil is ready, today could be the day!
Daddy likes to plant the corn in April or in May.

Here is the planter, coming down the row.
Funny how it figures out where every seed should go!

The big, yellow boxes sitting up on top
are filled with tiny seeds, which will make up our crop.

The sun and rain are needed, although the ground looks bare.
Now that the corn is planted, it will need some tender care.

Sometimes I get busy, but Daddy stays alert.

He always knows just when the corn pops out of the dirt!

Daddy doesn't like when nasty weeds grow in his field.
That is why he has them sprayed - to make sure they are killed!

I guess they never knew our corn would almost touch the sky,
when they made that funny rhyme "knee-high by July!"

Corn stalks have mighty roots, which help them stand up tall.
This is good for when strong winds try to make them fall!

As the silks start to change, we know it's getting near.
When the stalk turns brown, harvest time is here!

Before we start to cut the corn, before we even try,
Daddy goes and checks the ears to make sure they are dry.

To harvest all our crops, we use a big machine.
It is called a combine and it looks rather mean!

I ride in the combine, where my Daddy has the wheel.
He says, "Open us a snack" and I say, "That's a deal!"

Looking through the window, the corn head pulls the stalks.
Daddy pays attention, but I just sit and talk!

The auger arm comes out before the corn drops down.
Soon the driver's on his way to take the corn to town.

Here is where he'll take the corn - it's called an elevator.

He will drop it, load by load, so they can sell it later.

When we're moving right along and have no time to stop,
Daddy fills the wagon clear up to the top!

If we want to store the corn, we'll put it in a bin.
That is where it stays until my Dad says when.

I'm so proud of my Dad and all his hard work shows,
but for now another harvest season must come to a close.

As Daddy makes his final round, I'll try to hold my tears,
for when he says, *Goodbye, Corn*, he'll cut his last few ears!

Now we'll wait for winter's chill to come and go as planned.

In the spring, when the soil's right, we'll plant my Daddy's land!

CPSIA information can be obtained
at www.ICGtesting.com
Printed in the USA
BVHW021057110620
581241BV00003B/38

9 781614 932635